Bedtime Stories

A Collection of Short Stories for Children's Bedtime

Imogen Young

By reading this document, the reader agrees that under no circumstances is the author responsible for any losses, direct or indirect, which are incurred as a result of the use of information contained within this document, including, but not limited to, — errors, omissions, or inaccuracies.

Table of Contents

The Story of The Little Red Hen

Once upon a period, in a small farm there was a team of animals with no food to eat. Because they had been hungry, they chose to find a thing to cook. The little red hen discovered a wheat seed and rapidly requested for help:

- Who'll help me grow this seed? Would you aid me, cow? - requested the white hen, kindly

- No! Not me. It's too hot today. – replied the cow, annoyed

- What about you, pig, will you help me? – asked the red hen, politely.

- No! Not me. It's too hot today – replied the pig, a bit bothered

- Will you help me plant this seed, dog? – begged the red hen

- No! Not me. It's too hot today – replied the dog, indifferently

- Ok, then. It is settled. I'll do everything myself. – said the red hen feeling upset

And so the little red hen determined to raise the seed most by herself. After a few days, the sun disappeared and it began to rain. The little red hen decided, then, to go and check the garden:

- Who will help me collect the seeds? Will you help me to collect the seeds, cow? – asked the red hen, kindly

- No! Not me. The weather is too pleasant to do any kind of work – replied the cow, indifferently

- What about you, pig, will you help me collect the seeds? – asked the little red hen, courteously

- No! Not me. The weather is simply too nice today to do some kind of work – replied the pig, annoyed

- Will you help me collect the seeds, dog? – asked the hen full of hope

- No! Not me. The weather is too pleasant to do any kind of work – replied the dog, a bit bothered

- Fine. I'll do everything myself. – said the red hen feeling upset.

So the little red hen, once again, went all by herself to collect the seeds. As the weeks went by, the sun helped the wheat ripen, and soon it was ready to harvest. The wheat grew tall and strong so the little hen decided to ask the animals to help her thresh the wheat:

- Will you help me thresh the wheat, cow? – asked the little red hen, courteously.

- No! Not me. I want to rest within my barn today –
replied the cow, a bit bothered

- What about you, pig, will you help me thresh the
wheat?

- No! Not me. Today I don't feel like doing anything. I
want just to rest in the mud today – replied the pig
while   yawning

- Will you help me thresh the wheat, dog? – asked the little red hen, ever so kindly

- No! Not me. I want to rest in my comfortable kennel today – replied the dog, annoyed

- All right then. I'll do everything myself – said the red hen feeling upset

No one wanted to help the little hen, so once again she did everything herself. She threshed the wheat. When she completed, she asked her friends to support her to grind the wheat to generate flour.

- So then, which one of you would like to help me grind the wheat? Would you help me to grind the wheat into flour, cow? – asked the little red hen , kindly

- No! Not me. It's time for me to milk – replied the cow

- What about you, pig, would you help me grind the wheat into flour? – asked the red hen, politely.

- No! Not me. I am quite hungry. It's time for me to have dinner – replied the hungry pig

- Would you help me grind the wheat into flour, dog? – asked the little red hen full of hope

- No! Not me. I am quite hungry too; It's time for me to have dinner – replied the dog

- That's ok. I'll do everything myself. – said the little red hen, loudly

At this point, the little red hen ground the wheat into flour and then, she decided to knead it so she could have nicely baked good bread. Once again the little hen gave another chance to her friends and asked them for a little help:

- Who would like to help me in bake bread? Would you help me bake some bread, cow? – asked the little red hen, kindly

- No! Not me. I don't know how to bake bread – replied the cow

- What about you, pig, would you help me bake some bread? – asked the little red hen, politely.

- No! Not me. I don't know how to bake bread – replied the pig

- Would you help me bake some bread, dog?

- No! Not me. I don't know how to bake bread – replied the dog

- All right. Ill do everything myself – said the little red hen feeling upset

The little hen baked the bread all by herself and when it was ready, she let it cool down. Before cutting and eating the bread, the little hen looked around and saw no one:

- I wonder if anyone will help me eat all this bread – said the red little hen , loudly

- I will! – said the cow, enthusiastically

- I can help you too – said the hungry pig, happily

- If you would like, I could help you eat a bit of this delicious bread – said the dog wagging his tail

- No you won't! Said the little red hen - You didn't want to help me earlier so why should I let you try my tasty bread? This delicious bread is the reward for my hard work, so... I will eat everything by myself – replied the little red hen.

Scott and Nancy Learn to Get Along

Nancy and Scott are twins. They had spent their entire lives together. They liked the same foods, the same games, the same colors, and the same friends. For their short six years, they had gotten along amazingly, but one-day, things changed.

Ever since their sixth birthday, Nancy and Scott had started liking different things. At first, it was simple things. Nancy decided she didn't like peas anymore, and Scott decided he preferred the color green instead of the color blue. It wasn't a big deal. But then their differences became bigger. They got so big that Nancy and Scott didn't know what to do.

"No! She's my best friend," Nancy shouted at the top of her lungs.

"She gave ME the train for MY birthday!" Scott shouted back.

"It was MY birthday party, too, and she gave ME the remote-controlled car."

"Nuh, uh! That was ours. I was the only one that got something special."

"NO! YOU! WEREN'T!"

Nancy and Scott had screaming matches like this often now. What used to be a quiet household with twin siblings who could always find something to agree on was now a house of yells and screams. They couldn't find a middle ground anymore. One of them usually had to be correct, regardless of what. These fights might go on for hours in case their parents did not step in.

Cara and Brian, their parents, couldn't figure out what to do. They had sat them down time and time again explaining how to find common ground, and that it was okay not to always agree. But none of those meetings had ever helped. The twins seemed to be getting angrier and angrier with each other. Their parents were afraid that they might end up having a physical fight if they didn't learn how to get along with the changes to their personalities. Unfortunately, this present fight wasn't at home. It was in the park, and there wasn't anybody that could step in and stop their yelling. The park was only down the street from the house of theirs, therefore they were permitted to go there by themselves so long as they let their parents understand. They'd left only after noon, apparently in a great mood, and stated they would be home by 4.

It was well past four, and Cara was getting worried. She was sure they were okay, but with the way they behaved, she worried that they had gotten into a fight. She was just about to walk down to the park when the phone rang.

"Hello," Cara said.

"You need to do something about your kids," a shrill old voice stated on the other side of the line.

"Excuse me? "

Cara knew the voice. It was old lady Whittaker. She lived right next to the park, and she was always giving her "advice" about the twins. Ever since they had started arguing more, Mrs. Whittaker would call, and in her nicest way possible, tell Cara or Brian to make their kids shut up. She wasn't the nicest person, but Cara had learned to deal with her.

"Your children are at the park making a big scene," Mrs. Whittaker sneered.

"I was just getting ready to go get them, but thanks for slowing me down."

"I just thought you'd love to know that your kids do not understand how to behave in public."

"Thank you, Mrs. Whittaker. Goodbye."

Cara hung up the telephone. She grabbed her pursed and also raced out the doorstep towards the park. This was not the very first time she'd to pick them up from the park since they have into an argument. It'd happened almost every time they'd long gone to the park together after the birthday of theirs. As she got closer into the gate, she could hear them screaming.

"I need to invite her over for a sleepover, & I do not need you at home," Nancy screamed.

"I should invite her.. for a sleepover, & I do not need you at home," Nancy screamed.

"NO! I'm having a sleepover, and she's coming, and you're not going to be at home!"

Nancy was taking a deep breath to yell something back at her brother when Cara stepped in.

"Both of you home, now."

She motioned for Nancy to leave first and for Scott to follow her, keeping herself between them. They walked home in silence, but Nancy and Scott were still filled with anger. Once home, Cara sent them to their rooms to let them cool off. After a few minutes, she went to Nancy first.

"Why were you two making such a scene at the park? "

"Scott wants to invite Susan here for a sleepover, but she's my friend. I want her at my sleepover, and I don't want Scott here."

"When your father and I said that you two could have a sleepover, we meant together. Now, if you want to invite friends and he invites his, you and your friends can sleep in here and his in his room, but you won't be able to have a sleepover if you two can't learn to get along."

"But mom…"

Cara left Nancy's room and walked across the hall to Scott's.

"What were you and Nancy arguing about at the park?"

"She thinks Susan is her friend, but she is mine. She gave me a unique present for my birthday."

"You both got a present from her on your birthday."

"No, the train was mine, and the car was both of ours. "

"Scott, the package with the car had Nancy's name on it. You two can share it like you have done with toys in the past, but just like the train was given to you, the car was given to Nancy."

"Susan likes me better!"

"I understand that you're upset, but I don't like it when you yell at me. Like I told your sister, you two will not be having a sleepover until you can show me and your father you can get along for more than a few minutes and reach an agreement on the friends."

Cara left Nancy and Scott in their rooms. She felt angry herself, now, but she knew screaming at them wouldn't help. Instead, she went to her room and took some deep breaths and calmed herself. After a moment, she called Brian and asked him to bring in supper. She had some thinking to help her kids, and she didn't have time to cook.

Nancy paced around her bedroom. She still felt so angry with her brother. Ever since their birthday party, almost every day, she felt angry with him. When he spoke to her, she could feel her face going red, and her palms would begin to sweat. She never knew what to do, so she always yelled. Yelling made her feel good for a moment. She'd eventually calm down, and there were even times where she and Scott would get along, but that didn't happen often.

Scott was pacing as well. As much as he and Nancy had changed, they still had a lot in common. They felt just as strongly about each other. They both loved yelling when they were angry because that was the only thing that made them feel better. But Scott had an urge that Nancy hadn't experienced. He felt like he needed to hit something. He had never acted on it, mainly because it scared him.

When Brian got home, he set the table as his wife told him what had happened today. He shook his head. He missed the days when his kids got along, but they were two different people, so they had to learn how to accept each other. Cara called the kids in for dinner. Nancy and Scott ran into each other as they stepped out of the rooms .

"Watch where you're going!" Scott shouted.

"You ran into me!"

"No, I didn't. You had your door open first and waited for me to step out before you came out."

"Nuh, uh."

"Kids," Brian yelled, getting their attention, "That's enough. Get to the kitchen and sit down. I do not wish to hear more arguing."

Nancy and Scott walked to the table, hitting, and shoving each other with their elbows. Cara pointed to the two chairs across from each other. They sat down and frowned at one another. They knew what was going to happen. They were only sat across from each other if mom and dad were going to try to teach them a lesson. But Cara and Brian didn't say anything. They served up the food, and everybody ate quietly. The only sound that could be heard was the sound of forks on plates. Once everyone was finished, Nancy helped her mom clear the table. The kids started to leave the kitchen to go play, but their parents stopped them.

"Sit back down," Brian said sternly.

The children did as they had been informed and also sat back down. Cara had acquired a few big pads of paper and some markers and sat one down at each kid.

"We're going to do something and try to figure out why you two keep arguing, okay?" Cara said.

"Okay," the kids mumbled.

"Alright, I want you both to write down five things that the other does that upsets you."

The children quickly wrote down their five things and looked up to their mom for further instruction.

"What did you write?" Cara asked Nancy .

"He's tall, he likes the color green, he thinks everything is his, he doesn't like the pool, and he talks funny."

"Okay, Scott, what did you put?"

"She thinks Susan likes her, she hates peas, she likes dolls, she wants to take dance, and she likes to read."

"Now, write five things that you like about each other."

Nancy and Scott started writing things down, but it took them a little longer to get to five things. Their likes didn't come as quickly as their dislikes.

"What did you get, Nancy?"

"He eats the peas I don't like, he yells at the guys that won't let me play cars, he sings, he likes cats, and he's my brother."

"Scott? "

"She eats the carrots I don't like, she shares her toys, doesn't let kids laugh when I won't get in the pool, she helps me read, and she's my sister."

"Why did you two end with she's my sister or brother?"

"I couldn't think of anything else," Nancy said.

"Me, too."

"But that means you two still like being siblings, so why do you always argue," Brian said.

"Because she likes stupid things," Scott said.

"So, do you," Nancy stated.

"We're not arguing right now. You two want to have a sleepover?"

"Yes," they said .

"Then we have to figure out how you two can get along without fighting."

"Your differences are what make you two angry with each other, right?" Cara asked.

"Yes."

"Well, everybody is different. You get along with your friends, and they don't like the same things that you like, do they?"

"No, Susan likes playing soccer, and we both hate soccer," Scott said.

"But you two are fighting about who gets her at your sleepover."

"I suppose, but we can't both have her. And he is always trying to make me share something that I don't want to," Nancy said .

"Okay, I think it's time I told you, kids, something. You know Mrs. Whittaker?"

"Yeah."

"I don't care for her. She is always calling over here telling me how to raise you two, and how I am too soft of a parent. I don't appreciate how she always dismisses my parenting."

"But I never hear you yell at her," Nancy said.

"I know, that's why I'm telling you this. I don't yell at her because it wouldn't do any good. Sure, yelling makes you feel good for a moment, and it can help when somebody isn't listening to you, but most of the time, yelling isn't worth it. People listen better if you just talk to them. There is something about humans where we shut off our ears when somebody yells. There are going to be different people around you your entire life, and you have to learn how to work with them so that you aren't constantly angry. "

"Being angry will happen, but you don't want to be angry all the time. By the looks of it, you two have been angry almost all the time since your birthday. Anger can cause a lot of problems if you let it stay inside of you," Brian added.

"But how do we do that?" Scott asked.

"Well, you can always come to us, and we can help you talk it out, but we might not always be available to help. So, the first thing is, if you feel yourself getting angry, you need to go to your room. Take a minimum of 10 minutes to relax and when you do not really feel as angry, come back again, and speak to one another. Furthermore, it helps in case you label the emotions of yours. Nancy, you stated you do not as it as he acts like things are his."

"Yeah."

"How does it allow you to feel as he says a thing is his?"

"Mad. "

"Okay, when he does something like that, instead of yelling, say, 'Scott, it makes me mad when you say that something is yours.' This lets your brother know how you feel. You can also do that when he makes you happy or another positive emotion."

"I think I could do that," Nancy.

"Me too."

"Now, how are you two going to have a sleepover without fighting?"

"We could just have it together," Nancy said.

"Yeah, we could do like we always do, and our friends can choose who and what they want to play with."

"We could sleep in the living room."

"Yeah, and make forts with the furniture."

"Yeah, mama, daddy, could we do that? "

"If you go this whole next week without having a screaming match, yes, we can make forts in the living room," Brian said.

The kids jumped up and also hugged the parents of theirs. They felt lighter than they'd in some time, and neither one felt furious when they examined the other person. There have been times when they desired to yell and scream at one another during the following week, though they did not. They talked items through in a regular voice. Of course, there have been instances when they have some obnoxious, though the parents of theirs will step in and ask them to have a deep breath.

By the conclusion on the week, they aided their parents create forts in the living room before their friends arrived. Their entire sleepover was successful, and they never as soon as yelled at each other in front of their friends.

Melinda The Mermaid Minds

Melinda Mermaid was very excited about the upcoming party that Sally Snapfish was going to have. There were going to be some very important people there and Melinda knew that she needed to be on her best behavior.

But the party was next week and Melinda was getting ready for dinner with her family. They sat down for dinner at the table and began to eat.

"Hey give me the veggies." Melinda barked out

"What?" her mother exclaimed. "We don't ask for things like that young lady you know better."

"Sorry, Mom, can you pass the veggies please" Melinda corrected herself.

"Much better, you need to remember your manners for the party." Mom replied

Dinner got finished and Melinda was helping do dishes. "Buuuurp!" Melinda let out a large burp and laughed .

"Melinda, that is not very ladylike and I'm sure that the people at the party don't want to hear that!" Melinda's Father said.

Melinda finished the dishes and went to get ready for bed. She was brushing her teeth and didn't wash the sink out when she was done.

"YUK!" her sister yelled, "Melinda left the sink a mess. Melinda didn't think it was a big deal and just walked away.

In the morning Melinda sat at the breakfast table slurping her milk.

"Melinda, can you please not slurp your milk?" Mom asked, "That is not very nice and makes a horrible noise that we don't want to hear."

"Sorry mom," Melinda replied.

The party was getting closer and Melinda began to think about all the silly things she had done that were not very good manners and she went to her mom and asked her to help her learn how to act at a party.

She began by learning how to greet people. "Always say hello, Melinda, make eye contact and smile." Mom instructed. "It makes people feel welcome and relaxed. Next, let's talk about how to sit at the table and enjoy the meal with the other guests." Mom continued, " When you sit at the table you should not put your elbows on the table and slump over. It makes people feel like you are not interested in what they have to say. What they have to say is important just like what you have to say."

Melinda was already feeling better about going to the party.

"Keep going, mom." Melinda encouraged

"You should put your napkin in your lap when you start eating. This way it is handy to wipe your face and hands if you need it. When the drinks come drink slowly and try not to slurp. That noise can be very loud and people want to enjoy hearing others talk and slurping may be too loud for them to hear."

"This is great stuff mom, what's next?" Melinda sat up eager to hear more.

"When the meal is done make sure you put your napkin on the table next to your plate and if you decide to get up just say, 'excuse me for a moment please'. This is good so no one thinks you are just rudely getting up and walking away." Mom kept sharing, "When you are talking to other people, don't burp."

Melinda giggled. "Ok I won't "

"I'm serious Melinda, you think it's funny here at home but other people may not think that." Mom encouraged Melinda.

"When I am ready to leave, mom what do I do?" Melinda asked

"When you are ready to leave you make sure you go over to the person throwing the party and thank them for inviting you and telling them you had a good time and telling them goodbye." Mom finished her instructions.

This all sounded very interesting to Melinda and she felt ready to go to the party.

By the time the party day came, Melinda was ready to go because she had been practicing the things her mom had taught her.

There were many people at the party and Melinda remembered the things her mom had taught her. She enjoyed the party and felt like a young lady. She was setting a good example of good manners and when it was time to go to her friend's mother, she pulled Melinda aside and thanked her for being such a good-mannered young lady. This made Melinda feel good and she left the party happy.

The next day when she got home from school her mom asked her to sit at the table because she wanted to talk about the party. Melinda thought about it and thought things went so well what could her mom possibly want to sit down and talk about- that sounded serious. "What's wrong mom? I thought the party went well. I remembered all the things you taught me and Mrs. Snapfish even said I did a good job." Melinda said sitting at the table worried.

"Well Melinda, Mrs. Snapfish called me today to tell me that she thought you were a very well-mannered young lady who was happy to have you at the party." Mom said proudly. Melinda smiled her biggest smile and clapped her hands.

"I am always proud of you and who you are but it is always good to hear that other people see how great you are and feel like they need to tell us."

Mom shared and she sat up in her chair with a smile on her face. "Melinda a well-mannered person is always a joy to have around and I am so proud of you," Mom said and she reached over and hugged Melinda. "Minding your manners is always a good thing to remember, keep up the great work."

Melinda smiled and was very happy that she had learned all the good manners and was able to make other people happy by using them.

I'm Sally

Sally Atkins was only 10 years old when she learned that her parents were not getting along well. One night, as she was sleeping, she thought she was dreaming because, in her real life, there is only peace and harmony, but in her dream, there was calamity. She heard a man and a woman at first having a conversation, and then their voices became louder with much more anger in the sounds they made as they spoke to each other.

Sally got up early as she always had and made her bed, and then straightened up her room, also, as she always had. Sally was a model child, and in school, she was a model student. She loved her parents with all her might, and she loved her friends at school too. She even loved her teacher because she was taught at an early age to love those around her, and that's exactly what she did. She thought nothing of it and was certain that this is what everyone everywhere always did. It was just the right thing to do, and everyone knew it!

Each night, she had the same dream, and this was beginning to bother her, so one morning at breakfast, she waited until there was a space in the conversation her parents always had, and she spoke up. "Mother," she said in a clear voice, "I need to speak to you and Dad about something that is troubling me." She told them. "Oh, well, what is it, dear?" her mother responded with a smile. "Well," Sally said, looking down at her plate, "You know that I love you, right?" she began, and before her mother could respond, she continued, "And you know that I always do the right and good things every day." She said. "And I know that this is how you have always taught me to behave because it is just well, the right thing to do." And then, seeing that both of her parents had become solemn, and were now also looking down at their plates there at the breakfast table, she continued.

"I never have anybody unhappy around me, and I never cause anyone to be unhappy. I love the way my life is and wish to keep it that way, but there is something wrong, and I don't seem to be able to fix it." She told them. "What is it, dear?" her mother asked with a stern look on her face. "Well, it's just... I am having bad dreams, and I don't like them. I never have anything bad around me, as you know, as I have been saying, and this is a bad thing that is happening. What should I do?" she asked her parents softly.

Both of her parents looked at each other and then back at her, and then her father spoke up. "Sally, it would be alright if you would like to tell us about these dreams you are having, you know. We will always help you when you have any kind of problems in your life. That's a parent's job, to keep things running smoothly in the family and to make certain that when anything comes up, it is addressed, and we do it together as a family." He told her.

"Well, okay then, I guess I could tell you, but I don't understand why this dream is always the same." She said to her parents. "What happens is that I hear two people talking in my dream. A man and a woman. At first, they are just having a nice normal conversation, like this one we are having now, but then their voices become louder, and not very nice." Sally said, and then she paused. Nobody spoke, and both of her parents looked at each other with a look that she did not recognize.

Still, nobody spoke, so she continued to tell them about her bad dreams. "When the voices in my dream get louder, I can tell that they are getting more and more angry at one another, and I hate hearing that. I hate having to hear people when they don't love each other, and they don't get along like you have taught me is the right thing to do!" Sally was now crying, and her parents pushed their chairs back and came to console her. "Come now, honey," her mother said. "Let's go into the living room and sit together on the couch and talk this out."

By this time, Sally had composed herself, and she noticed the clock on the wall and needed to get ready for school. Her parents acted like they would have liked to talk further on the issue, but Sally, being the model child, she was, did not want to be late for school, and her parents respected this in their little girl.

In school that day, the teacher was beginning a new chapter in their social studies class. It was called "Being Mindful and Meditation!" This new information absorbed sally she was learning and couldn't wait to try meditating when she got home. "Now class, I am teaching you this chapter with a special wish that while we cannot give you homework on this topic, we hope you will follow the lessons in the book, and learn to meditate. I know that most of you already behave very well, which, in a way, is good mindfulness. Mindfulness is being in the moment and becoming more aware of your surroundings. It is also doing the right thing with those around you whether they are your family, friends, or even those you do not know or perhaps just haven't met yet." The teacher stated.

"Furthermore, meditation can be a very helpful tool for those who encounter problems or issues in our lives. It is not a "fix it" tool but rather a way to see the pathway ahead and know how to navigate life's obstructions and surprises." The teacher told them. Sally was delighted to hear this because she was well aware that she had arrived at just such an obstruction, and this might just be a huge help in understanding what to do about it.

When she got home that afternoon, she said hello to her mother, who was cooking for the family and then went straight up to her room to begin to study her new chapter. She read the entire chapter over twice to be certain that she understood this new thing. Then, she followed the suggestions in the book and knew that when it said to "find a good spot" to meditate, she knew exactly which spot would suite her needs. She had a window in her room that had a big soft bottom love sear across in front of it, and that is where she already always sat to do her homework and her deep thinking. She had a sudden thought; could it be that she had already been doing meditation without even knowing it?

She found her position and followed the directions. Finding the rhythm of her breathing and focusing her mind on clearing everything out of the thoughts. At first, this was difficult because random thoughts kept popping up and were a distraction. Then she remembered that the chapter had said that this would happen, and when it did, to just ignore these things and continue to see her "mind's eye." She worked her way through the things that she felt were not supposed to be what she was thinking about and soon found herself in a much more peaceful and tranquil area. This was indeed new territory for the little girl who had always been just the way the book said we should be. To do the right thing and to have peace and love in our lives. She loved how she felt, and she went deeper.

Before long, she heard voices in her head and thought, "Oh no, not again!" but soon realized that this was a part of the process, and it was a very good thing. She listened to what they were saying and repeated them into herself in her mind, so she didn't forget them after the meditation session.

Then it was over. She had done it! She had meditated

"by the book" and not coincidentally as she thought she might have been doing all along. As it happened, Sally was of the mind to be mindful in a very natural way, so it was true that she was, is a way, already in a meditative state at different times in the past. Now, she knew that, and she knew that this had ordered. It had a sense of purpose and intention now, which she loved. She knew that this was the beginning of something wonderful in her life, and she was very excited about it.

But what about her problem? How could she use this new medium to discover why she was having bad dreams, and even the same dream every night. She was certain that this was not normal, and normal was everything that Sally Atkins was. So, when bedtime came around again, as it always does, she said goodnight to her loving parents and went up to her room. Only on this night, she meditated again right before getting into her bed. She found her breathing and was easily able to get to the state she was for the first time. She heard voices again, only this time, she used her higher mind to speak back to them. To her amazement, she heard them answer her. She thought that it was like being on the telephone on she didn't need anything physical to communicate with other people. But who were they, where were they?

She finally finished up and got in bed. Before she fell asleep, she thought about asking the teacher why she could communicate with other people in her meditative state. She was very excited to learn the answer to this amazing question. Then sleep found her, and so did her dream. There they were again. The man and the woman speaking in low tones and then the energy levels rising and rising until they were both practically yelling at each other.

Then, what happened next was an occurrence that Sally would remember for the rest of her life. The voices in her dream had become so loud that she realized that these two people were yelling at each other now, and the experience in her dream was so terrible that she suddenly woke up, but the voices continued. They were the voices of her Mother and Father, who were fighting in the very next room. It wasn't a dream at all! It was real life, and it was worse than a dream. Her parents were no longer happy with their lives together, and she knew exactly what that led to. Many of her friends in school had a single-parent household because they couldn't get along and got divorced.

She couldn't bear to think of this happening in her own family and, eventually, cried herself to sleep. The next day, she waited until her classmates had all filed out of the class, so she was the only one left. It was just her and the teacher. The teacher noticed this right away, and Sally left her books on her desk, got up, walked over to the teacher's big desk, and began to explain her situation. She told the teacher the good news about how well she had been able to meditate and communicate with other people. Then she told the teacher the bad news about how she had believed that the fighting couple had been a dream. This is, until last night, when she woke up to the truth.

The teacher got up and closed the classroom door, and then brought a chair over for Sally to sit right next to her desk. "Sally, I cannot comment on your personal family affairs. However, I can comment on how meditation works and how you can use it at this time. That is our lesson this month, so I am obliged to do so even." She told Sally. Sally sat very still, stunned by everything that was happening to her and her teacher's huge kindness.

"This just must be one of the finest teachers in the world!" she thought as she listened to what the teacher was telling her. "First, I am finding it the highlight of my teaching career that you have this amazing gift. That is what this is Sally, a gift, and you are very fortunate to have such a gift. On that note, I will not attempt to guide you as you are already beyond my skill level and will find your way much quicker at this point without my help. However, I can offer some suggestions regarding your parents that is not advice and is still contained within the sphere of our school lesson plan. That would be simple for you to, in your way, try to get your parents to start meditating. Then, whatever their differences are, they would have the best chance of working their way back to staying a family. At least, Sally, this is what I would do if I were in your situation." She told Sally with a smile.

Sally thanked the teacher, and then they both noticed that each of them had a tiny tear running down their faces, and they hugged each other. That was another time that young Sally Atkins would remember for the rest of her life!

When she got home on that day, she knew she had her work cut out for her, and she had to get this right. "Do the right thing!" she kept saying to herself. Her Mom was again in the kitchen cooking, and when Sally walked in, she was bending over the oven, pulling out some muffins. She saw Sally and wiped her hands on her apron as she turned to greet her little girl. Sally knew that the only proper way to do this was to speak to both of them when they were together after dinner, but she thought, "it wouldn't be any harm if I told Mom about the school lesson." They both sat down at the kitchen table and had some nice Mint Tea and a hot muffin. The muffins were delicious, which was no surprise since her Momma had always been a great cook. Then Sally spoke up. "We have a new chapter in school, and it is on meditation. Do you know anything about that, Momma?" Sally asked her Mom. "No honey, but I have heard about it, and actually, I've always wondered what it would be like to try it." Her Mom said .

"I have started doing it, Mom, and guess what? I talked to my teacher and explained what if felt like, and she told me I had a gift. That's what she said, a gift!" Sally told her Mom. "And she also said that I was already way more advanced at it than even she was. Isn't that neat, Mom?" an excited Sally told her Mother. "Is that right?" her Mom said and leaned over to hug her little girl. "I love you, Sally." Her Mom said, "And your Father loves you too. You know that, right?" she told little Sally. "Yes, Momma, and I love you both right back, so you had better never forget that, okay?" Sally told her Mom.

Later after dinner, Sally made the announcement. "I would like to talk to you both about something and if we could just go into the living room," Sally asked them. "Why sure, honey," her mother said, and her Dad nodded his consent. Her parents took the couch and sat next to one another, but little Sally stayed on her feet. This surprised the parents as they had never seen their little girl so assertive. Then Sally began. "You must know that those voices that I thought I was hearing in my dreams were not in my dreams. I woke up last night and heard you both fighting." Bother of her parents nervously moved their legs at this news, but neither spoke, wanting little Sally to have the floor. "I don't want to talk about why you were arguing, but I want to offer some help. I spoke a little about this to Mom after school this afternoon, so she knows, but just let me tell you." Sally said, trying to keep her focus on the subject, and not let it get her into an emotional state. She realized that what she was feeling was mindfulness, and it was working for her.

"I think that both of you should learn to meditate and do it together. There may be a chance that you could work out whatever differences you have by doing this, and it would mean a lot to me if you would do this." Sally said. "That's it, that is what I wanted to tell you."

She said and then took a seat beside her Father, who grabbed her and hugged her. This turned into a great big group hug, and they all started to cry.

This was yet one more thing that little Sally Atkins would remember for the rest of her life. In the days that followed, her parents asked if they could borrow her textbook and taught themselves how to meditate. It must have worked well because Sally never heard them arguing ever again, and there was no talk about divorce. She had mixed feelings about what she had done but knew that everything that had happened led back to her. Her mindfulness and her love and caring for her family. It was true what they say.

The most powerful thing in the universe is Family!

The Lemur

"Today we are going on a hike," Leonard's troop leader announced. We need to listen carefully to directions so we don't get lost or hurt. All the members of the Tundra Team 24 gathered their backpacks and stood in line ready to go. That was Except Leonard.

"Leonard did you hear the Leader say it was time to go?" one of the troop members said poking Leonard in the arm.

"Hu? What? It's time to go?" Leonard said looking up from the bug he was playing with on the ground.

"YES, you need to listen. It's time to go." Another Troop member said.

They all gathered their belongings and headed out to the woods for the hike. There were so many interesting things out in the woods and Leonard was excited to look all over to see what he could see. They hiked for about 3 hours then stopped for a water break. It was a very hot afternoon.

"Let's stop here Troop." The leader instructed

The troop stopped and took out their backpacks and started eating snacks and drinking water. Leonard was so curious about the things around him that he didn't even think of eating something or taking a drink of water.

"Make sure you eat something and drink some water – We need to stay hydrated for the rest of the hike." One of the other Leaders said to the troop.

Leonard just kept wandering around looking at the light coming through the trees and at all the birds flying and bugs zipping around. He was so preoccupied with all that that he never even took a sip of water. After about 30 minutes of rest, the troop started again on the hike. Everyone was rested and had some energy because they ate a snack and had some water.

They hiked another hour and Leonard began to get weak. He began walking slower and slower. He started getting tired.

"I'm tired," Leonard called out.

"Did you eat a snack and drink some water at the last rest point?" The leader asked him.

"Uhhh, no? Was I supposed to?" Leonard said with a questioning ton e

"Leonard, hiking is hard and we take breaks to have a snack and drink water to remain strong. You must listen to what we say." The Leader explained.

Leonard stood there with a sleepy look on his face. Leopards were fast and had lots of energy but not Leonard, he was very tired.

"We will be stopping again soon so everyone please take a break, eat a snack and drink water." The leader encouraged again.

They all stopped up on the side of the mountain and there was a beautiful view. The members of the troop sat on the rocks, ate a snack and drank water. When Leonard reach the mountainside and saw the view, he was so excited and started looking at all the amazing views. He was so excited that he forgot to eat a snack and drink water again. Soon the troop packed back up and headed out. Leonard waddled along with the troop and after a few minutes into the hike he felt tired again.

"Oh no, I didn't listen again and I forgot to drink water and have a snack. I'm getting tired." Leonard mumbled to himself.

Soon the Troop reached the camp destinations and set up the tents and got ready for the campfire dinner. Leonard set up his tent and instead of joining the others he fell asleep because he was too exhausted from the hiking .

The other members of the troop sat and enjoyed a yummy campfire dinner, sang camp songs and had s'mores. They had a great time telling silly stories and sharing about things they saw along the hike. Leonard slept through all the fun the troop was having.

The next morning everyone got up and started packing up and getting ready for the hike back down, Leonard packed up his camp gear and looked over at the Leader and asked if they were going to have another campfire before they left missed out on all the fun.

"No, I'm sorry. We need to head back." The troop leader told Leonard. "But Leonard if you had snacks and drank water you would have felt better when we reached our camping area and could have hung out with the other members of the troop last night. You missed a good time. Maybe today you will listen when it's break time."

The troop headed down the mountain and decided to stop a few miles into the hike.

"Ok everyone, break time!" Called the leader. "Let's make sure to snack and hydrate!"

Leonard heard this time to eat and drink something and he did just that. He felt so much better when the group headed out for the next piece of the hike. The troop took a different route down the mountain and the next stop was at a large body of water where the Troop members got to rest and go fishing.

"Let's take a good rest here, drink water and have a snack and let's do some fishing!" The leader said excitedly.

The members of the troop were very excited to go fishing. Leonard was so glad he had listened to the other break time because this time he had lots of energy to participate in the fishing event. He even caught a fish before anyone else.

"Wow, look at me, "Leonard yelled to the Troop.

"So cool!" another troop member called back, "That's a big one!"

The troop finished fishing and packed up to finish the hike. When they reached the bottom of the mountain all their parents were waiting for them and couldn't wait to hear the fun hiking and camping stories they had to share. Leonard rushed over to his parents and grandparents who were waiting for him. He told them of the wonderful fish story he had. But he couldn't remember the camping night because he had slept through it as he had not kept up his energy on the hike up.

"Didn't you take breaks on the way up?" Leonard's grandma aske d

"Yeah, but I didn't listen at break time. I was too interested in the bugs and I didn't hear them tell me to drink water and eat a snack. I was too tired to stay up with the rest of the troop. I missed a good time." Leonard shared.

"Well, I am glad you listened on the way back. You sure have a great story about fishing." His mother chimed in.

"Yeah me too. Listening and following directions sure makes it easier to have a fun time." Leonard agreed.

The next weekend the Troop headed out for another adventure. Leonard was sure to listen and follow directions. Because he listened, he had the best time of his life, made great memories and had a great story to share when he got home.

Jurassic Friends

When things get difficult, a dinosaur can only look to their friends for help. When things get hard for us, we have to ask for assistance. And there's absolutely nothing wrong with leaning over a buddy from the time to time. Sometimes, we are not as lucky. But if you have friends, and in case they enable you to through tough times, then you're truly blessed.

We do not usually appreciate what he's until it is gone. This's why having friends seems common to us. When they're there, we love to play and laugh. But when they are not there, we think a bit of sad. And that is okay also. Do you've close friends? How many? Do you want to have numerous friends, and do you love to have just a couple of great friends? Take the time to think of who your buddies are. Just how did you see? What elements do you love to do together? And perhaps you have been there for them at the time of hard times? Have they been generally there for you? Friends are quite special to us. A good friend is much more important than getting a million dollars. friends that are Good just come one time in a life period. Friendship is a marvelous thing once you can feel it. You won't ever need to retturn to being alone. We've to look after our friends and be beneficial to them, because they're good to us in exchange. Occasionally a friend is going to need our help, and we've to offer it to them. Occasionally, a friend is going to need our support, and we've to offer it there. We've to be there for the friends of ours. It's such a lovely thing to possess friends do not you believe? Often large and strong dinosaurs require friends every sometimes. In Dino Land minor dynos go to college the same as you. They find out all their dyno facts and the way to live out within the big wilderness.

But several dynos are all by yourself. They've a tough time making friends since they're different. Or perhaps since they look funny to another dinosaurs. These dynos need to fit in together with the masses. Somehow, but who has learned. I want you to picture a wide open room, out inside the wilderness. Not the jungle, with numerous forests rather than the desert with just sand. Think of a room anywhere between. A place where dynos of various forms can collect and meet.

Dino school is very different from regular school. Dino's don't use pencils or chairs. They are too big for those things. Instead dynos sit and listen to what their teacher has to say. They don't have paper either. Everything that they learn has to go straight to their head. And you may not believe this, but dinosaurs have very good memory. Now take a few breaths to help relax your body. It is almost time for bed. I want you to fill your mind with good, happy thoughts about you and the friends you have made at school, at home, and everywhere in between.

Its okay if you have only a few friends. Or if you haven't made any friends yet. I promise you that friends will come in time. Even if we don't have friends, we can still imagine what a good friend may be like. Chances are, a good friend will be just like you. Or maybe they will be very different. It doesn't matter. Anyone can be your friend.

Sometimes, your mom is the only friend that you need. Your mama will always be there for you no matter what. And everywhere you look, some people love and care for you. It could be your dad, your brother or your sister, your cousin or your teacher. Someone somewhere out there cares about you.

And most importantly, you care about yourself. You love and care about who you are. You want only the best for you and your family That's why it is important to always believe in yourself. It is important to learn to accept who you are. And who are you? Well it all depends on how you look at it. Some people are short. Some are tall. Others are big, some are small. Some are strong, and others are skinny. People come in many shapes and sizes. And you know what? All of them are important. It doesn't matter what you look like. And it doesn't matter if you like reading books or if you like to play sports. Everyone is important in this world. But that is something that our friend Rexy the Tyrannosaurus Rex had to figure out on his own.

This is the story about Rexy and his friends. And it is a story of how one baby Tyrannosaurs learned to accept himself for who he was. Even the mighty T-Rex has problems with the way that they look. In Dino Land they are the king, the most fearsome dinosaur to have ever walked the earth. But deep inside, a T-Rex is just like you and me. They all have their worries, their problems and so on. And just like you and me, they care about how they look .

Now I want you to imagine the first day of school. The first day is always the scariest. You have to say goodbye to your parents for the entire day. For many of us, it is the first time we have to be away from them. And away from our house and our room and our toys. School can be very hard for some of us. Well in Dino Land it is no different, and early one morning Rexy the T-rex woke up to the sounds of his parents yelling at him.

"The sun is up the birds are out, and its your first day of school!" Said his dad.

"Wake up sweetie," said his mom. "Today is a big day for you"

But Rexy didn't want to go to school. He wanted to stay in his comfortable bed. Why did he have to go to school when he could stay home and chase butterflies all day? School was boring and a lot of work. He tried his best to stay in bed, but his mama flipped him over and made him stand up.

"You better wash and get ready," said his dad. "You don't want to be late on your first day of school, now do we? "

"No father," said Rexy.

Rexy washed himself in the nearby creek. Rexy figured that he didn't have a choice, and that he would have to go to school. He didn't mind the idea of school so much as he did getting up in the morning. Why did school have to be so early in the morning? If school started just a few hours later in the day, like after lunchtime, Rexy would go running to school everyday. He would have the biggest smile on his face. But no, instead he had to wake up at dawn and get ready in the cold. And washing wasn't the easiest thing to do when you are a tyrannosaurus Rex. With that big head of his and tiny arms it was a miracle that Rexy could wash himself at all. But he knew a little trick. All he had to do was dive into the water and scrape off the dirt using the nearby rocks. It was a hassle, but for Rexy the system worked out well. When he was all washed and ready, Rexy followed his mama and papa to the school grounds.

Rexy was looking forward to making many friends in school. He couldn't wait to see the new faces that would be there. School is a time for learning, but it is also a time for having fun. At school you are away from home. Your parents won't be there to watch over you. So you must learn how to get along with others there.

School also teaches you how to make friends. It is truly an awesome place once you think about it. There's nap time, free time, and Rexy's favorite, snack time. So if you can get over waking up early in the morning like Rexy did, school is just another adventure waiting for you.

"How do we know when we get there?" asked Rexy. "He was still very small compared to his parents, so he couldn't see very far. But his mommy and daddy where big, and they were tall. They could see for miles and miles. And they had big holes in the front of their heads for better smelling. If a T Rex couldn't see you, they could probably smell you. Especially if you smelled tasty.

"Not too far now, Rexy" said his mommy. "We are just about there. I can already see the fence. Rexy walked with his parents and almost fell over with every step. A grown up T Rex makes the ground shake wherever they go. And here Rexy was in the middle of two of them .

Rexy could smell the other dinosaurs before he could see them. There were lots of smells that he didn't recognize. As they got closer, he could hear the voices of all the baby dynos there waiting their first day of classes. Rexy and his parents went up a small hill, and below that hill they could finally see the other dinosaurs waiting behind the fenced area.

"You see those dynos down there?" Asked his mom. "Those dynos are your new class mates. So, make sure to say hello to all of them"

"And remember son," said his dad. "In school we cannot eat other dinosaurs. Am I clear? This is the best school on this side of Dino Land, and they only allow meat eaters under one condition. You cannot eat the other students".

Rexy said that he understood, and that his parents had nothing to worry about.

"Good," said his dad. "We can't get any closer than this, Rexy or the other parents will gets scared. This is where we say goodbye "

"Wait. You guys are leaving?" said Rexy a little scared.

"Rexy, we talked about this," said his mamma. "We can't follow you into school. They don't allow meat eater grown-ups like us"

"But mamma--"

"Go on now, Rexy." said his dad. "At the end of the day we will show up on this hill to pick you up. Do you understand? We will be here once classes are over"

Rexy's parents left him all alone on the hill. At first he was scared, and he even started to cry to a little bit. But that all changed when two Triceratops started to walk towards him. They were small—just like him. Where those his classmates?

"Hi!" said the green triceratops. "My name is Sarah. And this is Billy my brother. You must be Rexy!"

"Yep! I'm Rexy", he said .

"Then you can be our friend!" said Billy the brown Triceratops. "Come on, the others are waiting. Teacher said that school is going to start soon!"

Rexy walked with Billy and Sarah and met up with the other dynos. Once they were all inside the fenced area the parents started leaving one by one. Rexy saw them hug his classmates as they went and he felt a little sad. He still missed his mommy and daddy.

There where so many different dynos there that Rexy didn't know what to call who. He knew the two triceratops Billy and Sarah that said hi to him earlier. Apart from them, there where another three triceratops.

He also counted two duckbills, three flying dinosaurs, and one long neck. There was another dinosaur with spikes all around its back, but Rexy didn't know what kind of dinosaur he was. There were other dinosaurs too, but Rexy was too nervous to try to name them. As far as he could tell, he was the only meat eater there. It made him feel a little bit alone. All the other plant eaters seemed to have at least one pair. The long neck was the only other dinosaur that was alone like him. But even a baby long neck is already a very big dinosaur. And this one could squash rexy like a bug. Their teacher was an old looking triceratops named Mr Dandelion. He got that name because his favorite food was the dandelion, and that's what everyone called him. When Mr Dandelion cleared his throat, all the other dinosaurs stopped talking and listened.

"Hello all," said Mr Dandelion. "Today I see some old faces and some new faces as well. Whoever you are, welcome to another school year here in Dino Academy. Today I would like all of us to get to know each other first."

Each dyno had to walk up to the front of the class, say their name, what type of dinosaur they were and finally say what their favorite food was. One by one the plant eaters went up and said their names. Rexy was so nervous he thought that the world was going to end. His heart went ba-dump, ba-dump ba-dump.

"My name is Sarah!" Said the green triceratops from before. "I am a type of triceratops. And my favorite food is cabbage!"

"Nice to meet you Sarah," said the rest of the class at once. Sarah smiled at everyone and then sat down in her spot.

"Okay let's see here," said Mr Dandelion. "Ah. The next student is a new face here at Dino Academy. Can Rexy please come up to the front and tell us a little about themselves?"

Rexy heard a bunch of whispering behind his back as soon as his name was called. His claws where so sweaty that he didn't know what to do with them. He felt like the entire class was looking at him.

"Uh hello," he said to the class. "My name is Rexy and uh"

From the corner of his eye Rexy saw that Sarah and Billy where giving him a thumbs up a big smile. That helped him a lot.

"My favorite food is seafood!"

"Nice to meet you Rexy!" Said the rest of the class.

When Rexy went to sit down his new friends Sarah and Billy where still giving him a big thumbs up. After introducing himself, Rexy didn't feel so scared anymore. Maybe school could be fun like his parents said. After the introductions, Mr Dandelion introduced them to the first school subject called memory skills. It taught dinosaurs how to remember things. Dinos don't have paper, so they have to remember everything. Mr Dandelion told the class that it took him only five minutes to memorize the entire class, their faces and their favorite food. Rexy was amazed that his teacher remembered everything, and he wanted to be just like him.

After memorization skills the dynos were introduced to counting, and Rexy was very good at it. Rexy had grown up counting things all on his own. He counted how many hairs his dad had on his forehead and the number of dinosaurs at the lake. One time Rexy even tried counting the number of scales on his body, but he couldn't do it without losing track of which scales he already counted. Rexy was surprised to find out that he was one of the best students in his class. He never raised his hand, but he almost always knew the answer. Even when nobody else would know it, Rexy wouldn't say anything. I wonder why that was? Rexy was a T-Rex and T-Rex dinosaurs are not afraid of anything. Usually it's the other dinosaurs who are afraid of the T-Rex. But there is another thing that has been bothering

Rexy. Something that he heard the other dynos talking about. Sure, Rexy was different from them. But Rexy was also strange looking. And the other dinosaurs didn't like it. One of the things that Rexy overhead them say was that he had little arms. Ever since they said that, Rexy didn't want to raise his hand anymore. Even if he knew the answer, because he knew that the other dynos would laugh at him. When Mr. Dandelion dismissed the class, all of the dynos walked to their friends. Rexy didn't know who to sit with, so he just stood there listening to the others talk.

"Did you see those arms?" Said the dinosaur with spikes on his back. "They look like twigs!"

"Tyrannosaurus Rex?" said a duckbill, "more like small-armasaurus"

The other dinosaurs that gathered around them started to howl with laughter.

"Don't listen to them," said Sarah the triceratops. "They are just bullies, that's all"

"You can sit with us Rexy," said her brother Billy.

But before Rexy could say anything he saw his dad standing on the hill from before.

"Thanks guys, but I have to go"

Rexy walked by the group of dinosaurs making fun of him and he heard their laughter explode as he passed. Rexy felt like he was going to cry. But since his dad was there he didn't want to look like a weakling"

"There's my boy!" Said his massive dad. "How was your first day at school?"

"It was okay" Said Rexy.

He did not talk much about how home and his father knew something was wrong. It was not like Rexy to help keep quiet.

"Son, did something happen at school?"

"It's nothing dad, really"

But his father wasn't having any of it. Rexy saw his dad flare his nostrils in anger.

"You tell me what's wrong right now, or I will go back to your school and have a word with your teacher"

Rexy gulped. He knew if his father went over there and argued with poor old Mr Dandelion something bad would happen. Knowing how his dad got when angry, Rexy thought he might even eat Mr Dandelion. And Rexy didn't want that, because he liked Mr Dandelion. And so, Rexy told his dad everything about what happened at school that day. About the name calling, the laughing, and being embarrassed about raising his hand in class.

"Well this won't do," said his father, "This won't do at all Rexy. Your education comes first. Who cares what those plant eaters say to you. You can't let them bother you "

"But they do bother me, dad," sad Rexy looking down at his tiny arms. "Why do I even bother having arms if I can barely use them?"

"Son you are a T Rex!" Said his dad snapping his mouth and showing his teeth. "We have small arms.

But we also have powerful jaws. And we have strong legs. We can outrun almost any plant eater out there, and you want to be sad about little arms?"

"What should I do"? Asked Rexy. "If I go back to school tomorrow they will just laugh at me again"

"Well you are still going to school mister!" said his dad. "I got an idea"

His dad put his enormous head next to Rexy's and whispered something in his ear.

That night Rexy went to sleep feeling a little bit better. And after hearing his dad's plan, Rexy was ready to confront his bullies. A T Rex never runs away. And a T Rex never lets somebody make fun of their little arms. When Rexy showed up to school he was full of confidence. His dad told him a trick, and that trick was simple. The only way to deal with bullies is to bully them back. Rexy's dad said he used the same trick when he was small to respect him. Well, when Rexy tried it the plan didn't go so well. During recess all the dinosaurs were having fun and playing, but Rexy waited for the perfect time to strike. He found his target, and he lined up for an attack.

"Hey you with the spikes!" Said Rexy to the Stegosaurus who was making fun of him yesterday. "What does it feel to be a peanut brain!"

Everyone gasped. The stegosaurus looked at Rexy then back at his friends and then at Rexy again. And then they all burst out laughing.

"Peanut brain!"

"Did you hear what he said"

"He said peanut brain!"

As the dinosaurs howled with laughter Rexy saw that they weren't laughing at his jokes. They were laughing at him.

"You plant eaters are all the same!" Said Rexy. "All roar and no bite!"

But the other dinosaurs kept laughing at Rexy. His dad's plan didn't seem to work and now he didn't know what to do.

"Why I ought to..." Said Rexy, but a loud cough stopped him from behind him.

"Mr Rexy," said his teacher, "Can I have a word with you in my office?

Uh oh. Was Rexy going to be in trouble?

Mr Dandelion didn't have an office. He just pulled Rexy aside so that the other dinosaurs couldn't hear what they were saying .

"Rexy," he said. "Our school is very strict about name calling and bullying. I don't want to hear you saying bad things to the plant eaters again"

"But--" said Rexy.

"I want to remind you," his teacher interrupted. "That you are a minority here. The parents of the plant eaters were very nervous when I told them that a T Rex would be studying. Because of this, you have to be on extra good behavior. You have to set the example. Do you understand?"

"Yes Mr Dandelion," said Rexy.

It just wasn't fair, thought Rexy. Why did he have to get in trouble when it was the plant eaters who had started everything. They were the ones that were bullying him.

"Don't worry about them," said his friend Sarah the triceratops. "If Mr Dandelion sees them bullying you he will talk with them too "

"My sister is right!" Said Billy. "You have to focus on your school work and not let the others distract you"

But Rexy wasn't so sure. Every time he raised his little arm somebody always started laughing at him. How was he supposed to ignore them and focus on his school work then? He wanted to show Mr Dandelion that he was a good student who paid attention in class. But the others kept distracting him.

"Hey Rexy, do you want to play tag with us?" Asked Sarah when the school day was over.

"Okay!" Said Rexy. It was the first time he was invited to play since starting school. And he liked to play tag. A T Rex is quick on their feet and one of their favorite activities is chasing things.

"Tag you're it!"

Rexy started chasing after his new triceratops friends and he was having a blast. They were pretty fast for plant eaters. But they weren't fast enough!

"You are it!" Said Rexy

It wasn't long before the other dinosaurs got interested in their game of tag. First a duckbill asked to play, and then another triceratops. Soon half the entire class was playing with Rexy and his friends. Some of his bullies watched from afar.

"Look at the T Rex!" One of them said. "He can barely reach with his little arms!"

Rexy pretended not to hear them, but the others started laughing. And he was having so much fun too. Rexy was really glad when he saw his mom waiting for him on the hill. He said goodbye to all his friends and ran home.

"How was the day of yours at college, honey" Asked the mom of his.

Rexy told her all that had occurred, and also just how utilizing his dad's advice did not work.

"Don't tune in your dad!" Said his mom. "It is not alright to intimidate others, even in case they're being mean for you. You cannot fight fire with much more fire. It simply does not work "

"Then what should I do?" Asked Rexy. "They won't stop making fun of me, even when I am having fun"

"I have an idea sweetie," said his mom. "But I can't promise it will work"

Rexy listened to her idea, and he thought it was genius. He couldn't do anything to make his little arms grow, so all he had to do was get bigger arms! His mom helped him look for a big stick, and helped him wrap it around his little arm with vines. Then she did the other arm as well. When she was all finished, Rexy's new arms were much bigger than his old ones. He could reach for things easily. Rexy loved them, and he couldn't wait to show them off at school the next day.

The pieces of wood made noise when he walked, but he didn't care. He was so happy to have new arms that he ran to school, clopping all the way. He must have looked a little ridiculous, but Rexy only cared about having longer arms. Rexy showed up to his school with the new arms. At first nobody noticed them, but after a while dinosaurs where staring at him.

"What are those?" Asked Sarah.

"Oh, these are just extra arms my mom made me. They are so I can reach things!" Said Rexy.

"Aren't those uncomfortable?

"Not really!" Rexy said.

"I think they are cool!" Said Sarah's brother Billy.

Now when Rexy raised his hand he didn't feel bad about using his little arms. He could reach high up in the sky. But his new arms had lots of problems. It was tough for him to sit down on the lawn, and he kept bumping into some other dinosaurs and poking them in their faces. By the conclusion of the day everybody was laughing at him once again. He looked a lot more absurd than before. And now he was bumping into another pupils, he was creating a huge commotion.

"Ouch which hurt!" Said one terrible duckbill which Rexy accidentally struck with his rubber arm.

"I'm going to inform the parents of mine about this! "

Another dyno nearly got his eye poked away by Rexy's arm whenever they had been playing tag.

That is when Rexy heard the common cough behind him. Uh oh.

"Rexy." stated Mr Dandelion. "Can I've just a little talk with you?"

"You ca n't bring all those arms to classes anymore, Rexy. I am sorry but they're simply too a great deal of a distraction for another pupils. If I see them once again tomorrow I am going to have to confiscate them"

Rexy was heartbroken. He was beginning to love his latest arms also, and today the teacher declared he could not take them to school. "Now what am I meant to do" thought Rexy. His dad's plan did not work. And today his mom 's idea had also been from the question.

Rexy walked home with the dad of his that day being sad.

"I offer up!" He said. "I'm likely to stop college and join the circus!"

"You will not be performing that," stated his dad. "I worked tough get you into this particular college. You'll be staying"

"And the bullies?" requested Rexy.

"We will simply have to contend with them son. There needs to be an additional way"

"But we previously attempted everything!" Rexy said. "Nothing appears to work!"

"We will simply have to consider something different. Do not quit Rexy"

Rexy spent the majority of the day attempting to cope with the bullies at college. Though each time he considered something, all he might consider was another pupils laughing at him. Or maybe Mr Dandelion informing him he could not do it. But then Rexy got a concept was remarkable. His plan was so good he could not wait to check it out. His plan was very simple. The other dinosaurs did not like because he was very different. So all he'd to carry out was be much more like them. He'd to be as a plant eater. If a plant eater appreciated eating grass and trees, and then as would he. If a plant eater appreciated to sit around all day, and then as would he. And if a plant eater appreciated making fun of various meats eaters, and then as would he. Rexy was extremely excited going to school the following day and try out the new idea of his. The first thing he'll do is eat grass with the veggie eaters and present to them he may enjoy them. The only issue was what Rexy had never tasted grass before.

"Good morning Rexy," said Sarah.

"Morning Sarah, morning Billy" Said Rexy.

Then without warning, Rexy stuck his face in the grass and started eating it just like the triceratops did.

The grass tasted terrible, but Rexy was determined to be just like them.

"Rexy stop!" Said Sarah. "You can't eat grass like us. Mama said you will get sick" But Rexy said that he felt fine. He said that he liked grass, and that he was eating grass ever since he was born. "I'm just a little different, that's all" said Rexy. "I'm not like other T Rexes"

As the day went on Rexy continued to eat more grass. The other plant eaters looked at him curiously. What was he up to? It was the 1st time they saw a T Rex eating like them.

"That meat eater is eating plants," they would say. Or, "That meat eater is crazy"

"He's not a real plant eater unless he eats dirt!" Said the stegosaurus.

And that is exactly what Rexy did. He walked over to the river where the dirt was very muddy and he shoved a mouthful of dirt into his face.

"Yummm," he said.

The other dinosaurs couldn't believe their eyes. They laughed so hard at Rexy for eating dirt that they almost started crying.

It looked like his plan had failed. The other dinosaurs were laughing at him harder than ever.

When it was time to go home Rexy had a terrible stomach ache.

"Well did you eat something funny," asked his dad.

Rexy explained everything that had happened at school that day, and told them about his idea to become a plant eater. "That's not possible, son" said his dad. "Once a meat eater always a meat eater"

"I just wanted to be more like them. So they wouldn't make fun of me anymore for being different"

"It's okay to be different, son. We can't all be the same, can we?"

"Rexy," said his mom. "Sometimes the key to bullying is to simply be yourself "

"What do you mean mama," Said Rexy. "What do you mean be myself?"

"What I mean Rexy, is to go to school and just be you. Who cares if you have little arms. Or if you eat meat. Having little arms doesn't mean you can't be smart"

His mama was right. Rexy knew he was one of the smartest in the class. He always knew the right answer, but he was too embarrassed to raise his hand.

"You are a T Rex," said his dad. "You should be proud of that"

"I am proud!" Said Rexy. "And I do like being a T Rex!"

"So, then you should be also proud of having small arms," said his dad. "Because that's how T Rexes are made"

His dad was right. T Rexes have small arms, but that doesn't stop them from being one of the coolest dinosaurs.

"Okay," said Rexy. "For now on I will be myself at school. Thanks mom, thanks dad"

Unfortunately for Rexy, he would have to pay the price for trying to be a plant eater. He'd a tummy ache for the whole day. Show and tell was coming up in school and Rexy wasn't sure what he would take. He couldn't take his wooden arms, because Mr Dandelion sad he couldn't bring them anymore. Instead Rexy decided to bring a shiny rock he found the other day by the river. The rock was his favorite color of blue just like the sky. The other students brought many different things. One duckbill brought in their pet giant cricket, and another came in with their favorite stick. The triceratops brother and sister brought in really big feather. The long neck dinosaur brought in a necklace made out of twigs. Each dinosaur took turns talking about their favorite thing. When it was Rexy's turn, even his bullies listened to him talk. Everyone liked his shiny rock. And he let them take turns looking at it. Overall, it was a really good day. And all Rexy had to do was be himself. He didn't let anyone bother him. He raised his hand, even though it looked funny .

"Oh no!" Said the stegosaurus. "I can't find my great-great-great grandfathers spike!"

The stegosaurus had lost his show and tell item. The dinosaurs all helped look and look, until finally one of the duckbills spotted it.

"Is that it? There, in between those two boulders!"

"Yes that's it!" Said the stegosaurus. "That's my great-great-great grandfathers spike!"

The only problem was that no dinosaur could reach it. There wasn't enough room to reach a hand down there. Rexy was interested in what they were doing over by those two boulders. And even though the stegosaurus used to make fun of his arm, he still wanted to help.

"What's going on here?"

"Nobody can reach the spike," said the duckbill. "Our hands are too fat and stumpy! "

Ah, but not Rexy's. Rexy's arm was short and small. It fit perfectly in between the two boulders.

He pulled it out without any help from the others and they all watched in amazement

"Wow! You did it" said the Stegosaurus. "I guess T Rexes aren't so bad after all"

When Rexy's mom came to pick him up on the hill, he told her everything. Nobody called Rexy names after that, and they never laughed at him for having small arms.

"You were right mom. I just had to be myself and everything worked out!"

The next day Rexy woke up extra early to go to school. He couldn't wait to meet up with all his new friends. When he got there, they surprised Rexy with a gift.

"Here you go Rexy," said Sarah. "I know it's hard for you to raise your hand in class, so we got you this" They made Rexy his very own hand! Well, not really. It was just a big stick with a wooden hand attached to the end. Every time Rexy wanted to answer a question in class all he had to do was pick up the stick high up in the air After that, nobody made fun of him for having small arms again. In the end things ended up well for Rexy. And all he'd to carry out was be himself. Everybody has the unique way of theirs of doing things and everyone differs. You have to figure out how to recognize those differences since you are the reason you. A meat eater could not turn into a vegetable eater, and that's acceptable. Several individuals are created with great noses, others have curly locks, and some are only somewhat different from everybody else. But much like Rexy learned, it's alright to be changed. Therefore do not hesitate to be yourself. Being yourself is actually that you can be. And with that, the friend of mine, I want you a goodnight. I'm happy you decided to stay with me throughout this adventure we'd in Dino Land. And I am very happy you have to meet Rexy and most of the friends of his. I am hoping you enjoyed it almost as I did.

Until next time.